THE
TROUBLE
WITH
WORDS

Identity and Language

John Simmons

Newell and Sorrell

For Matthew and Jessie
who have their own way with words

Acknowledgements We thank the following for the use of extracts reproduced in this book. Dennis Potter, quoted in *The Guardian;* David Ogilvy, for *The unpublished David Ogilvy,* published by Sidgwick & Jackson; Gabriel Garcia Marquez, for *Love in the time of cholera,* published by Jonathan Cape; Anthony Burgess, from *Earthly powers,* published by Penguin; Penguin Books, for their editions of *Nostromo* by Joseph Conrad; David Kusnet, from *Speaking American,* published by Thunder's Mouth Press; Keith Waterhouse, from *On newspaper style,* published by Viking; visual examples from Sherratt & Hughes, Waterstone's, Lumino, The Body Shop, ITPS, Routledge, InterCity, Parcelforce, Robinson.

© Newell and Sorrell Limited 1993

No part of this publication may be reproduced, stored in a retrieval system, or transmitted in any form or by any means, graphic, electronic, mechanical, photocopying, recording or otherwise without prior permission of Newell and Sorrell Limited.

Newell and Sorrell Limited, 4 Utopia Village,
Chalcot Road, London NW1 8LH, United Kingdom

Introduction

Switching on two copiers one morning, I waited for them to warm up. I stared at them. Two different brands, yet they looked more or less blandly the same. I waited as they whirred and hummed. Suddenly and simultaneously, they both woke up and writing appeared in their tiny control panels.

"Ready", said one. "Start", said the other. At last, I thought, a point of distinction. Different company ideologies and different products with different attitudes to me. One ready to serve and the other inviting me to use it. I was curious. How did the two words get chosen? Were they simply the results from two translators of Japanese, or were they chosen with skill to affirm real differences in corporate identity and product design. I concluded it must have been pure chance.

Of course they would have made more sense if the "ready" machine was programmed and fully automatic, and the "start" one was manual. But people don't yet use words as integral aspects of product design. They certainly don't use language consciously as one of the most powerful means of expressing a corporate identity.

With more power to move people than corporate symbols and icons, words are an under-utilised resource. Misused they can create misunderstanding, misery, disappointment, even havoc and terror. Used effectively they can create inspiration, clarity, entertainment, relief and delight.

In this wonderfully written book John Simmons will inspire you to think again about words, to appreciate them with a sharp consciousness of their power and to use them as the most effective and accurate tools that exist in our universe.

Michael Wolff

Beginnings

One of the things I do - rather too haphazardly - is jot down in a notebook either thoughts that occur to me about writing or phrases that I come across and like. A little while ago I wrote down this phrase I'd seen in a newspaper...

"The trou
words is
know who
they've

ble with
you never
se mouths
been in."

I really liked that phrase because it expressed a truth in a witty way. We are all 'green' with words - we recycle them constantly. The trick is not so much to find new words but to find new ways of saying the old words.

The truth of the phrase was also brought home to me when I started preparing this book because I could not remember who the hell had said it. Days passed and it was nagging away at me. Then one Sunday evening a sudden flash of remembrance struck when the TV announcer said the following...

> **Viewers are warned that the next programme contains explicit language**

The next programme was Dennis Potter's *Lipstick on my collar* and it is to him that I owe the title of this book, which I have also adapted as a running theme. The quotation I had originally noted was from an interview with Dennis Potter.

But let's just pause for a moment on this TV announcer's phrase. What it means is that some viewers might be offended by swear words. However, it doesn't say that. Viewers might actually prefer an explicit warning.

THE TROUBLE WITH WORDS IS THAT THEY DON'T ALWAYS SAY WHAT THEY MEAN.

If I'm talking to myself it doesn't particularly matter if I don't know what I'm talking about. But if I want to communicate - to get across to another person the thoughts I have in my head - then the imprecision of words starts to become a problem.

However, it's a good starting point for us all to understand that words don't necessarily communicate what we hope they will communicate. That's why I've always been interested in the combination of written and visual messages to strengthen meaning.

> *"If everybody in our company took an exam in writing, the highest marks would go to the 14 directors.*
>
> *The better you write, the higher you go in Ogilvy & Mather. People who think well, write well."*

When I came across this statement a couple of years ago I didn't know whether to laugh or cry. For as long as I can remember I've used writing to sort out my thinking, and to explain this to people I have said 'People who write well, think well'. And there was David Ogilvy's version in print, a good demonstration of the trouble with words, you never know whose mouth they've been in, I'd been beaten to the phrase.

Except that, in this case, I don't mind at all. David Ogilvy, as a writer for business, is one of the great writers of the century.

David Ogilvy started life as a salesman. He wrote a guide for door-to-door salesmen on 'Selling the Aga Cooker'. It starts ...

> "In Great Britain, there are twelve million households. One million of these own motorcars. Only ten thousand own Aga Cookers. No household which can afford a motorcar can afford to be without an Aga."

That's the start. It goes on for a dozen pages. It's brilliant. It also illustrates an important point about writing - it seems to me an inescapable principle that good writing is about selling.

sell

I've given talks to help people write better proposals and business reports, to write better blurbs for book covers, and to write better letters. In each case the writer is trying to convince the reader to 'buy', although the exchange of money is not always essential to this buying process. The principles also apply to poetry or novel-writing. The important point is that between the buyer and the seller, the reader and the writer, a relationship needs to be built. Without that relationship there is no hope of a sale. You can call it advocacy if you like, or the argument, but it is selling in the sense that the writer is trying to persuade, convince and win someone over.

You don't always succeed. I'll be using a few examples from American politics in this book, but this one might be the only one I agree with.

"You agree with me on 9 issues out of 12, vote for me.

You agree with me on 12 out of 12, go see a psychiatrist."

Mayor Ed Koch

"The past is a foreign country: they do things differently there."

From The Go-Between by LP Hartley

"It is a truth universally acknowledged, that a single man in possession of a good fortune, must be in want of a wife."

From Pride and Prejudice by Jane Austen

"It was love at first sight.

The first time Yossarian saw the chaplain, he fell madly in love with him."

From Catch-22 by Joseph Heller

Perhaps the first principle of selling and writing is to seize attention. This starts with the very first words and it's a writing skill that I have long been fascinated by.

For example, for Sherratt & Hughes we designed a series of bags which used opening lines from novels. In selecting these for the bags, I was actually voting for my three favourites. The three I chose were by Joseph Heller, Jane Austen and LP Hartley. Each immediately establishes the book's tone of voice and starts to build that necessary relationship between writer and reader.

Tone of voice is all-important, as Keith Waterhouse pointed out in his book, originally written as the house style manual for the *Daily Mirror* in the days when it employed journalists. You can substitute the name of your company for the *Daily Mirror* and the words are still relevant.

> *"...Does all this matter? Yes. Every word that appears in the Daily Mirror, from the splash headline to the most obscure clue in the Quizword, has a byline - the byline of the Daily Mirror. The pitch of the Mirror's voice reveals what it thinks of its readers. The voice-range runs from respect (the Mirror at its best) to apparent contempt (the Mirror at its worst)."*

But let's stay with opening lines, because they offer revealing insights. This is from *Moby Dick*.

Call me Ishmael

You are immediately addressed in the most startling way. You back away but there's no escape. You're confronted with a real person.

> It was inevitable
> that the scent of bitter almonds
> always reminded him of the fate
> of unrequited love.
>
> Love in the time of cholera — Gabriel Garcia Marquez

A more subtle approach from Marquez, immediately establishing his novel's tone of regret, and through the use of key words - inevitable, bitter, fate, unrequited love - straightaway introducing the book's themes.

> It was the afternoon of my eighty-first birthday,
> and I was in bed with my catamite when Ali announced
> that the archbishop had come to see me.
>
> Earthly Powers — Anthony Burgess

Here Anthony Burgess is really making a joke of the novelist's challenge to write a dramatic opening. How many shocking thoughts can you cram into one sentence?

One final example of opening lines from John Donne.

> Sweetest love, I do not goe,
> For wearinesse of thee.

> For Godsake hold your tongue,
> and let me love.

> Busy old foole, unruly Sunne,
> Why dost thou thus,
> Through windowes, and through curtaines call on us?

Although written 400 years ago, and in verse, the easy conversational tone immediately catches your interest and establishes that vital relationship between writer and reader, or perhaps more revealingly between speaker and listener. Note too the use of questions to engage you, another useful technique.

The other important point to demonstrate from looking at literature - and the way books are marketed - is that we constantly bring different interpretations to great books. Each age reinterprets a book in the light of changing history, taste, pre-occupations. This is why it's possible to read a great book again and again. In the words of Ezra Pound, on this poster we designed for Waterstone's, 'Literature is news that stays news'.

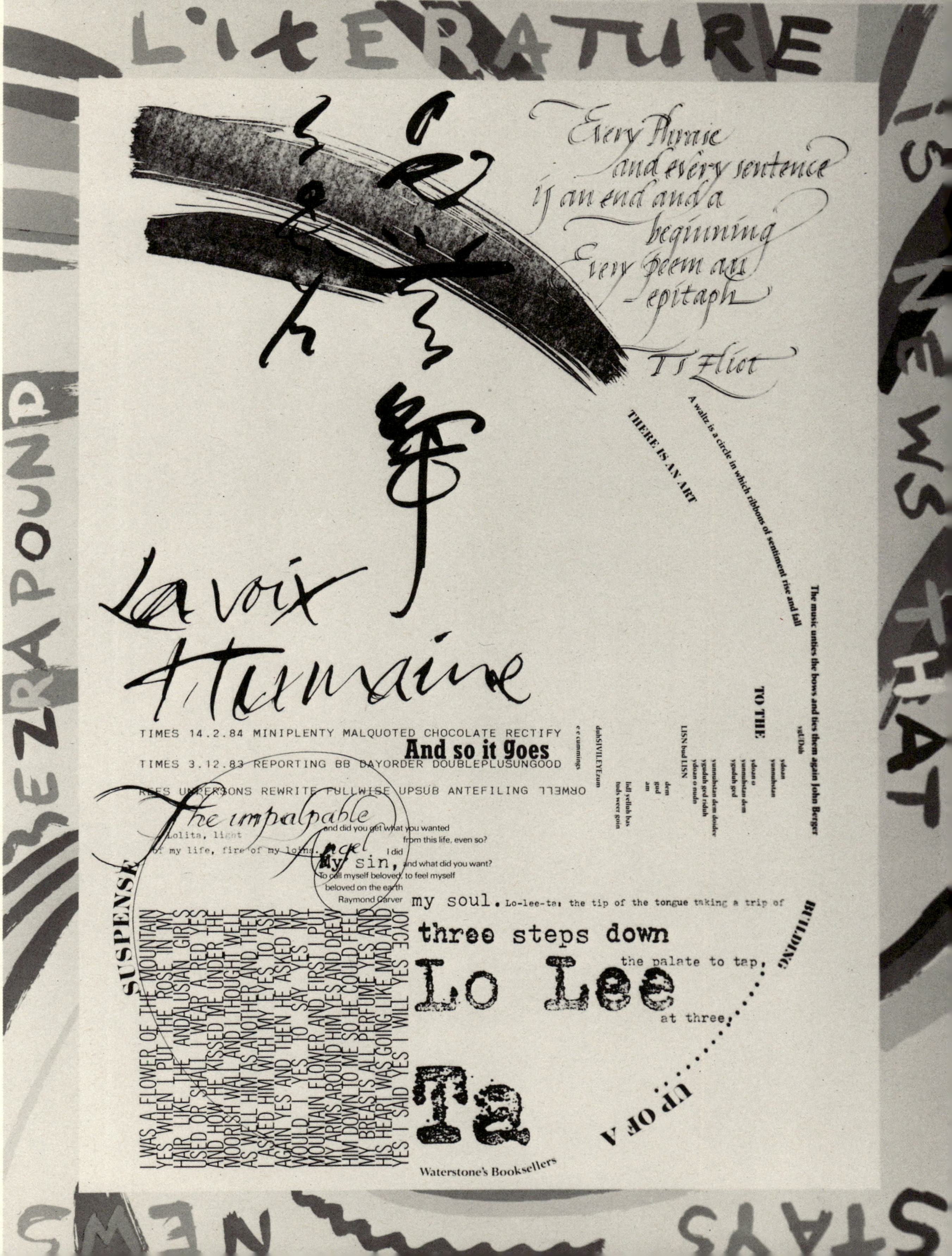

L'ITERATURE IS NEWS THAT STAYS NEWS
EZRA POUND
Every Phrase and every sentence is an end and a beginning Every poem an epitaph
TS Eliot
THERE IS AN ART
A waltz is a circle in which ribbons of sentiment rise and fall
The music unties the bows and ties them again John Berger
TO THE
La voix Humaine
TIMES 14.2.84 MINIPLENTY MALQUOTED CHOCOLATE RECTIFY
And so it goes
TIMES 3.12.83 REPORTING BB DAYORDER DOUBLEPLUSUNGOOD
REFS UNPERSONS REWRITE FULLWISE UPSUB ANTEFILING ORWELL
e e cummings
The impalpable Angel
Lolita, light of my life, fire of my loins. My sin, my soul. Lo-lee-ta: the tip of the tongue taking a trip of three steps down the palate to tap, at three, on the teeth. Lo. Lee. Ta.
and did you get what you wanted from this life, even so? I did and what did you want? To call myself beloved, to feel myself beloved on the earth
Raymond Carver
SUSPENSE
BUILDING
UP OF A
I WAS A FLOWER OF THE MOUNTAIN YES WHEN I PUT THE ROSE IN MY HAIR LIKE THE ANDALUSIAN GIRLS USED OR SHALL I WEAR A RED YES AND HOW HE KISSED ME UNDER THE MOORISH WALL AND I THOUGHT WELL AS WELL HIM AS ANOTHER AND THEN I ASKED HIM WITH MY EYES TO ASK AGAIN YES AND THEN HE ASKED ME WOULD I YES TO SAY YES MY MOUNTAIN FLOWER AND FIRST I PUT MY ARMS AROUND HIM YES AND DREW HIM DOWN TO ME SO HE COULD FEEL MY BREASTS ALL PERFUME YES AND HIS HEART WAS GOING LIKE MAD AND YES I SAID YES I WILL YES JOYCE
Waterstone's Booksellers

For example, let's take these two versions of a Penguin classic, *Nostromo* by Joseph Conrad. The version below shows the front cover and part of the blurb of the edition published in 1967.

> Amid
> the grandiose scenery
> of South America,
> against the exciting
> events of a revolution,
> Conrad ironically
> displays men,
> not as isolated beings,
> but as social animals.

In 1967 we thought of South America in terms of its grandiose scenery. Revolution (or the idea of revolution) was exciting, and people (although no doubt individuals) were seen within the context of society.

Below are shown the front cover and blurb of the edition published in 1990.

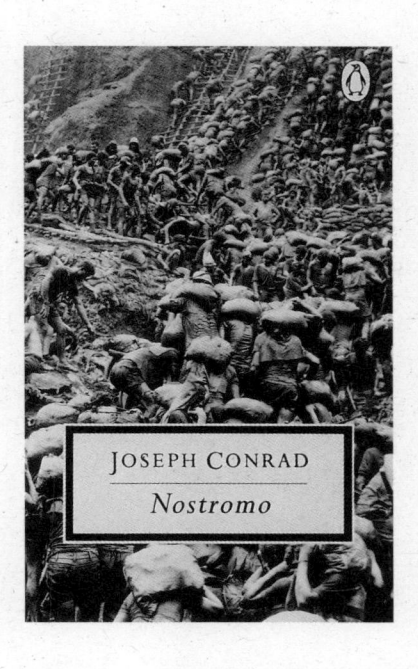

> The novel captures the tragic and brutal essence of Latin-American politics as each character's potential for good is turned to corruption or defeat.

By 1990 South America is seen somewhat less romantically. Politics - closely associated with corruption - can defeat the individual and the individual's potential for good.

If we stay with Conrad, he wrote *Heart of Darkness* at the turn of the century, questioning the colonial experience in Africa in a way that no European had previously done.

By the 1970s Francis Ford Coppola had taken *Heart of Darkness* as his inspirational starting point for a film about the horror of Vietnam. Each age reassesses its own experience in its own language which reflects that experience. You need to see writing in context and that applies to any kind of writing.

FRANCIS FORD COPPOLA
PRESENTS

Apocalypse Now
X

Middles

Having established a context for my own words, let us now look at some particular points to do with language.

There is no such thing as a correct use of language. Words need to do too many things for us ever to be able to say, ah that's the only one. Of course our aim will always be to invest words with as much meaning as possible. Words, whether or not by our own deliberate intention, are always trying to break free from tight chains of meaning.

It seems to me an amazing strength of the English language that we not only give words to other languages but we take in words too.

There is almost a trade in words which adds to the richness and diversity of language. Words are sometimes ambassadors, sometimes refugees, and often they find more natural homes outside their original environment.

For example, a Hindi word bungalow that conjures up an essentially English way of living.

Laissez-faire a French phrase that has no English equivalent so we have adopted it as the French have taken 'Le parking' and 'Le weekend'. But if, on the other hand, you compare passages of English written now and in, say, 1593 the differences would be enormous compared with the changes in French over that period. English is a language in constant and relatively fast evolution, and all the richer for that.

It's also a language of inconsistency and possibilities, particularly in its spelling. The illogicality of English spelling is another sign of experimentation and invention with language.

Though
Through
Plough
Rough

Tho Drive-thru Plow Ruff 'n Tumble

For example, we all recognise 'tho' as an abbreviation of 'though'. We understand the concept of 'Drive-thru'. We might well have a feeling in the back of our mind that 'plow' is an older (or possibly American) spelling variant. And thinking about 'rough' I looked up the phone book and discovered a company called 'Ruff 'n Tumble' which turned out to be a day nursery.

The possibilities of alternative spellings indicate the potential to create new forms of language. When we think of this we think particularly of America.

Dancin' broccoli heads
Ezi-cough
Shurfine
Shoprite
Nuway

Throughout the century the invention of brand names such as these has been closely associated with an American way of selling and marketing.

We have many examples in this country too, of course.

Kwik Save
Supawash
Kar Rite
Xpert Engineering
Xtra Hair

In this country there is perhaps an inherent snobbery in our attitude towards this kind of brand name. It's hard to create an upmarket brand or a brand that stands for quality when the name depends on a misspelling. For the English it's like a social gaffe. These names mean other things to us - cheapness, lack of sophistication, a basic level of service.

INVISIBLE **EXPORT**

There is another aspect to our use of the English language. It is perhaps our last asset as a nation. As we approach the next century, like an old banger with bits dropping off it, our language remains our greatest invisible export. It is the most international language of business and of knowledge, and it is the kind of import barrier and in-built export advantage that we imagine the Japanese would love to have invented.

It's not one that we can be complacent about, though. When Sony invented the Walkman, they were advised by their English-speaking marketing experts that the name 'Walkman' would never do. People wouldn't understand it. Instead they recommended 'Soundaround'. Fortunately Sony ignored this advice and the Walkman it was and still is.

listen

The best advice I can give is to listen. When you write, when you use English, either say the words out loud or say them inside your head. This simple practice would kill off most examples of bad writing - and therefore of bad thinking.

'For PC3 (writing) first examine the constituent AT levels,
based on the NC test levels and the TA level in the case of AT4/5.
If the TA in AT4/5 (presentation) is at level 7
and the NC test level for AT3 (writing) is at level 8,
then the PC level is the AT3 NC test level.

However, if the TA in AT4/5 is not at level 7,
but is higher than level 4, then the PC level is worked out as follows:
AT3 NC test level x8 plus AT4 TA level x2, divided by 10.'

This bad thinking, for example, comes from the Department of Education which was trying to get English teachers to test 14 year olds on their English language skills. Trying to read this, our sympathies are entirely with the English teachers who decided to boycott the test.

If one civil servant had read these words out to another I can't believe that they would have been printed. There is a beauty in words and we should never be ashamed to strive for that beauty.

"I put confidence in the American people, in their ability to sort through what is fair and what is unfair, what is ugly and what is unugly."

George Bush

The previous US President had a certain way with words. I found it absolutely fascinating that Bill Clinton had three equal directors of his Presidential election campaign team - one responsible for strategy, one for communications, and one (David Kusnet) for language. I like to think that the result of the election was partly a victory for language.

Words are invested with a power beyond their size. Let's take as a prime example the word...

B

IG

David Kusnet writes about the villain for the American people always being Big. "Big money, big business, and big government are all rhetorical whipping boys for populist politicians."

"The story of the California environmental referendum, 'Big Green', proves the point. As some commentators observed, the ballot measure lost 'not because it was green but because it was big'."

Although I suspect that the word green is now also seen through a veil of cynicism. It's a word and a concept that is too easy to abuse.

THE TROUBLE WITH WORDS IS THAT THEY HAVE A LIFE OF THEIR OWN.

There is a cultural difference there between the US and the UK. I think we're less sensitive to the issues surrounding 'Big' and perhaps the image of James Stewart going to Washington is less mythic for us.

But David Kusnet goes on to make an observation which we can apply to our own communication style in this country, and this lesson is certainly not confined to politics nor to the English language alone.

His observation was about the 1988 election, when in a scripted speech George Bush talked about his yearning for

A kinder, gentler America

The words are words that you would use to describe a real person. That is their strength, that's what gives them life.

They place an image before everyone who hears them that can be individually adapted to fit that person's experience. By contrast, Dukakis speechwriters, trying to say the same sort of thing, talked about 'a more decent, compassionate society'. It sounds benevolent but bureaucratic.

I invite you to apply the same analysis to your own companies. I've hardly mentioned businesses or companies up to this point, and that has been deliberate. I get excited by words and I get depressed by uniformity. I hate the way that companies exclude the animate from their language. There is, for example, a whole language of 'personnel' which denies the humanity which has to be at the heart of that particular function. 'Human resources' is a symptom of this kind of thinking.

A kinder, gentler WH Smith
A kinder, gentler Post Office
A kinder, gentler British Telecom

and so on...

WORDS CAN MOVE EXPLAIN, STARTLE, EXCITE, PERSUADE, EXPRESS IDEAS... AND MORE.

These words are words I use to express my own beliefs. I enjoy writing and I would love everyone else to enjoy it too. If you learn to love words you will automatically learn to write better.

Ends

For the final part of this book, let me try to narrow the focus to the use of language and corporate or brand identity.

Let me start with an example of the emotional power of words within a company's identity. The example is the United States Post Office building in New York. There is an inscription that runs across the building and which reads:

"NEITHER SNOW NOR RAIN NOR HEAT NOR GLOOM OF NIGHT STAYS THESE COURIERS FROM THE SWIFT COMPLETION OF THEIR APPOINTED ROUNDS."

Now there is something that strikes us as quaint and old fashioned in that. It almost needs Cliff Clayburn, the mail man from 'Cheers', to stand, hand on heart, and declaim it. But despite that it seems to me a beautiful, ringing and distinctive statement of the value of public duty. I would argue against any cynicism - the statement remains a wonderful vision of public service, a statement that expresses and engenders pride.

A lot of organisations try to achieve a similar effect with Latin mottos. Most of these have a genuine traditionalism which makes them acceptable.

PER ARDUA AD ASTRA
VICTORIA CONCORDIA CRESCIT
NIL SATIS NISI OPTIMUM

I doubt, however, whether we would identify strongly with a new company which tried to import a spurious tradition through the use of a Latin motto.

Sometimes, though, you can turn that to advantage. Lumino was a new name and identity for a company that was previously called HWS Contracts. HWS were the initials of the owner's name. When his sons came into the business, instead of installing electrical ring mains, they wanted to sell sophisticated Italian lighting to architects. But, of course, they couldn't do that while they were called HWS Contracts.

LUMINO

The name Lumino sounded right for an Italian lighting supplier. But it was an invented name, drawing on the Latin word 'Lumen' for light. If we went back that far, could we not go further? So Lumino - as our story went - was the name of the youth who was loved by the Goddess Selene in Roman mythology and, from jealousy, turned into a star. Pure invention, of course, but the story was completely swallowed by the design and architectural press and Lumino as a company got the best possible marketing launch.

Some companies have deliberately used a style of language that is unexpectedly partisan. The Body Shop has a distinctive visual style that we all recognise. But what I think drives that style is the company's campaigning stance which carries through everything it does. By proclaiming 'Trade not Aid' it sets a style of language, which demands a matching visual style, and it appeals to the social consciences of its customers to give them a different and distinctive reason for buying Body Shop products.

WHY WE ARE DIFFERENT:

WE RESPECT THE ENVIRONMENT *Reuse - Refill - Recycle*
WE ARE AGAINST ANIMAL TESTING FOR COSMETICS
Cruel - Unnecessary - Misleading
WE HAVE A NON-EXPLOITATIVE APPROACH TO TRADE
Equality - Employment - Trade Not Aid
WE MEET THE REAL NEEDS OF REAL PEOPLE
No Idealised Images - No Extravagant Claims
WE CAMPAIGN FOR ISSUES WE BELIEVE IN

> # *Good old fashioned Service*
>
> BROUGHT TO YOU BY MODERN TECHNOLOGY
> WITH A HUMAN FACE

Everyone now talks about customer service. For ITPS we helped the book distribution business of International Thomson to create a visual and written approach that acknowledged the fact that everyone is now talking about it. Through the approach we took we were saying, often in so many words, that customer service is not a new notion to ITPS.

A lot of the work we have done with Routledge on their identity has been to do with the use of language. We started by defining the company as inquisitive, questioning, keen to explore the byways as well as the highways of academic publishing. This led to a copy style that reflected this questioning approach, and which had the parallel aim of making Routledge books more accessible to booksellers and book buyers.

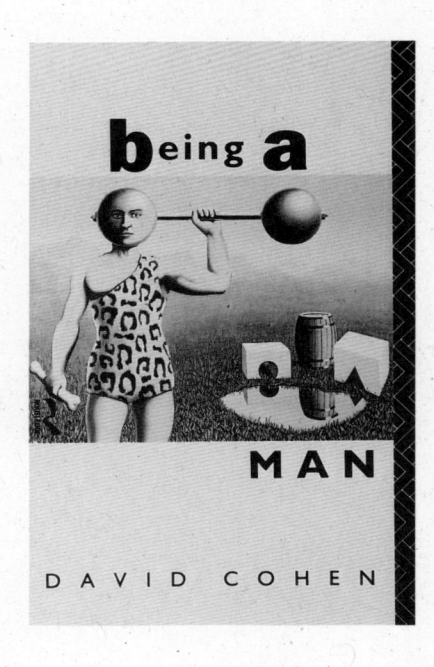

What is it like being a man today?

Has feminism had any real impact on men's lives?

For many companies, clarity of communication should be part of the brand. In a busy railway station or airport, or in the streets of our towns, clear and informative signing is a customer service. Sometimes this kind of helpfulness can go astray.

> **ATTENTION**
> WARNING, IF THE MARKED CAPACITY ON THIS LIFT IS EXCEEDED THERE IS A SPECIFIC DANGER IT MAY FALL DOWN THE LIFT SHAFT.

When we began working with InterCity our observation was that the InterCity visual language at the stations was the same as that used for directing people to the toilets. If the visual language needed to change, so too did the written language. It started with a simple statement of mission.

"InterCity is, quite simply, the most civilised way to travel at speed from city centre to city centre."

I particularly liked the use of the word civilised. With mission statements there is a seemingly irresistible temptation to use portmanteau words like 'best', 'quality', 'excellence'. Here was a different, surprising but still aspirational word. And again, like the US Post Office, it contained an idea of public service that suggested deep roots.

The InterCity copywriting guidelines followed the principle 'Less is more'. There are principles to abide by, not rules to follow. The only rule is for people always to think about the language they are using.

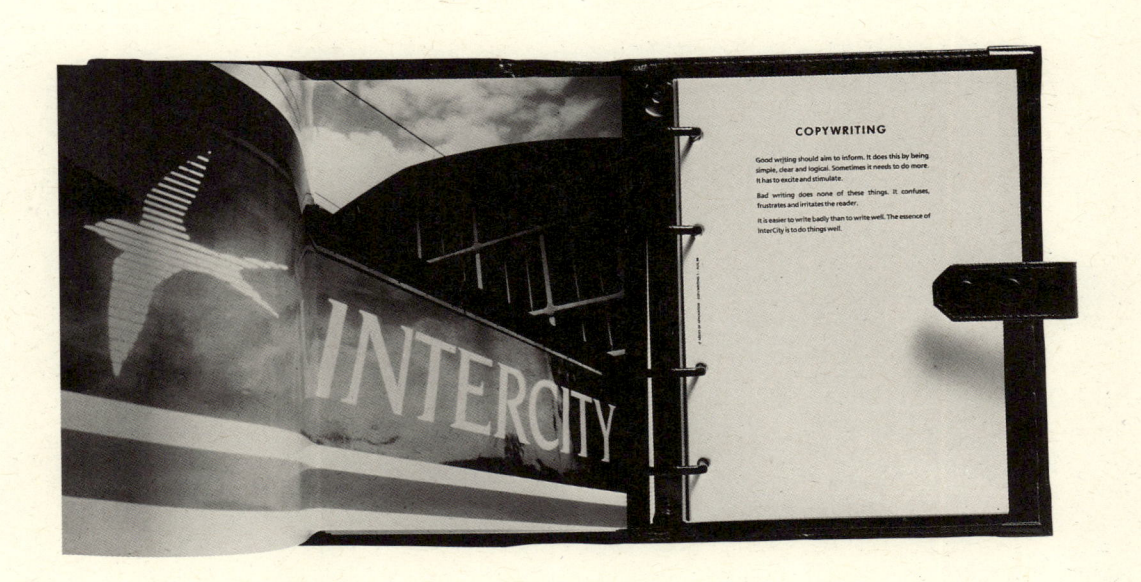

THE POWER TO DELIVER

Sometimes language - or a phrase - is used as a deliberate and identifiable basic element of an identity system. For Parcelforce our phrase was The Power to Deliver which I am happy to call a slogan, for a slogan originally meant a war cry. Parcelforce needed an aggressive and confident statement as part of an identity that would help them to compete more aggressively in their market.

ROB1NSON
CARE COMES FIRST

By contrast, our work for Robinson led to a much gentler, more caring phrase as part of this company's identity.

Around for over 150 years, manufacturing products for healthcare and packaging, Care comes first was used to express a quality commitment to people who worked for Robinson. It was also linked with the numeral 1 from the company logotype.

Other companies have other phrases. Some of them, through consistent repetition over many years, achieve instant recognition and identification with the company or brand. You will almost certainly know the companies behind these phrases.

We try harder

—

Never knowingly undersold

—

The world's favourite airline

—

Everything we do is driven by you

And it's more than probable that you will associate a brand of beer with this single word.

probably

This is probably the great triumph of twentieth century English copywriting - to invest a brand with qualities of excellence through the use of a single word, and a word that seems to claim nothing.

THE TROUBLE WITH WORDS IS ......

...THAT THEY CAN *RUN AWAY WITH YOU.*

We try very hard to control words but sometimes they do get out of control. Words are your children. Be aware of them, don't let them run riot while you pretend that they have nothing to do with you. They can inflict small, unthinking acts of cruelty on your neighbours.

> 'We have a problem
> of biological leakage'

This was said by the marketing director of the *Daily Telegraph* a few years ago. It referred to the problem of older readers dying off. I suggest that this is not the kind of language to use when thinking about any group of customers. It dehumanises them and stops you thinking about them as people.

> *I don't mind the prospect of growing old.*
> *Particularly when I think about the alternative.*
>
> Dave Allen

To take a serious point from a good joke, think about the alternative. In language, there always is an alternative. Avoid the hackneyed ways of saying things and try to produce words that seem freshly delivered.

Think about the words you use. I've talked about first words and arresting openings. Remember that you also need a good middle and a good end. A good end might be what Dave Allen meant by the alternative. But make sure you get to your conclusion and some memorable last words. Unlike General Sedgwick who raised his head above the parapet at the Battle of the Wilderness and said ...

Nonsense! They couldn't

hit an elephant at this dis